"TAPPING INTO YOUR SOUL'S ENERGY"

By Miss Kathy Tyrity, BSBA, Silva Mind Control Graduate

This metaphysical book was written in an environment of soul relax. So, first I would like everybody to do that – relax . . . take a few deep breaths. And the topic for the first lecture is "The Color Blue – It's Power; and the Medulla Oblongata."

Observe . . . in the center of the front of your neck (area of the thyroid gland) . . . visualize a diamond in the color blue. This diamond symbolizes Wisdom and Truth. This diamond will guide you on an inner journey with your form, regarding any subject. To complete any task, to see clearly, to observe now, the diamond of blue in that area. As you breathe in through your nose, concentrate on exhaling through the diamond.

Experience it now . . . There is no need to create anything, such as a vibration, atmosphere . . . it is only that you should create a still and stable body.

Ask mentally . . . your purpose for using the Light.

Sit for the count of two or three minutes, and then let go of the diamond of blue. If you choose at that moment to receive your guidance, then you may sit a while longer, but not necessarily will it come in that instant.

However, if your sit again at the same time of day, in your calm space, and repeat that question, you shall receive.

But don't necessarily expect to receive every time, instantly. Instead, know that the guidance can come in different forms . . . it can be personal, it can be inspirational, it can be consciously or subconsciously. There are many methods in which your own spiritual energy chooses to reach your consciousness and subconscious Soul's Nature.

Page Two – **Tapping Into Your Soul's Energy** – by Kathy Tyrity

This Diamond of Blue should only be used in times of deep need.

When you are wrestling with a problem, when you feel the need to touch into your Soul's Energy, when you feel the need to receive wisdom and knowledge . . . to move through a particular situation . . . you may use this Diamond of Blue for yourself. If you are feeling blue and out-of-sorts, or your term may be: "I feel (such and such) this, depressed." You may use it. It is the doorway to many of the energy patterns I will give you to help you to become more in touch with your very Nature, your Spirit and its Power.

As you know, this group (you and your friends) will learn how to deal with difficulty in a most calm and secure manner. There is no purpose any greater than your Spiritual Body . . . Do not ever feel as though you are all alone.

Do not ever feel as though you are doing wrongly. At times, you will see a need to participate with a great number of people – this is not uncommon. You cannot always stay only with those of like mind. You must be able to inter-act with the general world. You must be able to enjoy, perceive and have fun – at the same time using your Spiritual Values to live your Life.

You must not always be concerned with your Growth, but live your Growth through your own Personality.

Don't be afraid of making an
error, but BE AWARE of the
need to be aware . . . Therefore,
you will be able to throw away
Concern . . . For, if you are
concerned, you are not aware.

Think about it!

If you are concerned, then you
are not aware – For, CONCERN
is a powerful anxious energy,
and it hides and confuses
Awareness.

So, be at one with Yourself. Also, however, ENJOY life to its fullest and know that your Essence here on this Earth is not only to love and to help, but to enjoy and receive and be deserving of it.

Know that all things that will come to you will be powerful and loving and of the highest caliber.
Page Three – **"TAPPING INTO YOUR SOUL'S ENERGY"** – K. Tyrity

Is that not what you expect when you put your foot on a Spiritual Path? Then, do not deny it when you receive it. Be at peace with your Nature and know that there will be time . . . for everything. And that everyone that is in your Life is right and perfect. And that what you are doing is Right and Perfect . . . And, that where you will Go, you will know and I shall guarantee it!

And you must have the courage
and faith to approach life with
happiness and joy . . . and know
that, Spirituality is what your
ARE, not what you must create.
And what you ARE is
EVERYTHING. Yet, you place
too much Concern on minor
infractions of your life, instead of
recognizing that JOY can be
received – in many different
ways. And that, if you are
Concerned, then you are
overshadowing the everyday
gifts of Life and LOVE.

So, then, the basic message of this segment is to greet life with JOY in almost every moment – and receive back everyday, the gift of LOVE.

(END OF LECTURE ONE)

In your Nature, is also the power to SURVIVE . . . with Love and Strength and peace, and Harmony.

It is your Being. And you do not need to deny yourself its greatest Power.

So --- BELIEVE in yourself.

At the same time, create the motivation necessary to move onward. Did you get that. Create a motivation for yourself to move on. In my life, this can take a few days after a period of adjustment. Also I have found, it is very important to create motivation for everything in life. This actual book became my motivation to keep my mind centered after an eight-month investment of my time away from home. So I moved on to the next project. So it is.

Now, create your own motivation necessary (after your period of adjustment) to move on to your next project, the next energy outlet, the

Page 4 - TAPPING INTO YOUR SOUL'S ENERGY – By K. Tyrity

energy expenditure on something of value, or that needs to be done. . . in order for your Soul to move onward.

Believe in yourself, and at the same time, create your motivation necessary to move beyond this . . . to take one step and place it in front of the other. Instead of hanging back and waiting for things to be given . . . or to just happen.

You, too, must be a Creator of things and happenings in your own Life. You, too, must be the benefactor of those things and your own Energy, because you will like the result of a creation, an accomplishment or feat of your own action.

By the same terms, we ask . . .
How can you benefit if you
won't create or accomplish
something?

No, you must do something or
learn it or create, or accomplish,
with energy almost all the time.

So, don't go about it in an . . .
anxious way . . . rather, go about
it with JOY and in a SURE Way!

Careful consideration of your physical and emotional Nature . . . yes . . . but also careful consideration of your Spirituality through these daily energy expenditures on your projects of life. Otherwise, you would certainly not be reading this expenditure of my time.

Be at peace now, and know that your desire to manifest your Spiritual knowledge and your wisdom and your intuition and your . . . psychic power, or shall I say Intuition . . . that all of that is already existing in your life. Isn't that about how you came to pick this up this time?

And yet, everyday you may wonder, "Am I doing it right?" "Am I OK with this?" "Am I right?" "Did I say that OK?" "Did I do all right?" "Oh, will this ever all come to me?" "Will I receive what I need?"

Page 5 – 'TAPPING INTO YOUR SOUL'S ENERGY" K. Tyrity.

Well, in the long scheme of things, you already have it. So be sure and take your steps with assuredness. Learn from other people who are in "your same boat." Take mental notes. Don't be so concerned with 'being concerned' that you fake or fail to see the main play of the main cause. Know that these tools in this book -- to manifest your energy properly – are not given trying to excite you…but to help you live better.

You already have tools, but I want you to use them. They cannot do the work if you do not apply them. Intuition is a major key, or "psychic ability," and use it! In so doing, you ask the question to yourself, evaluate the answer, and pursue the Ideal – by Motivating the Self, in everyday accomplishment of your project or your work or your daily needs. And the energy created by knowing you MUST MOTIVATE, is a key Tool to recognize the task you have created, and ignite the Power to accomplish what you have now set out to do. And then you are . . . the Keeper of the Flame . . . the Keeper of the Temple . . . the

Power behind the Soul!

And, only YOU can complete
what you have chosen to commit
yourself to, from one project to
the other in this Reality.

So, don't be so concerned about
commitment . . . JUST DO IT! Be
happy with where you are now,
so that you can see that – What
you are now is just as perfect, as
what you are going to be. It is
just as loving. But if it is not as
loving as you wish . . . it makes
no matter; it is better than what
you Were.

Be SATISFIED . . . be
ACCEPTING . . . BE what you
are, and be happy with that! And
then all things will be given to
you, and I guarantee it.

Because we will take other
journeys in this exploration, and
because we will explore some of
space and travel outside
ourselves – None of that is half
as important . . . as your Nature .
. . your Spirituality . . . your
Spirit! The rest is for fun, for
interest, is for . . . excitement.

But, the expression of your Spirit
. . . is powerful . . . is satisfying
and complete. And that is what I
want you to be.

Pg. 6 "TAPPING INTO YOUR
SOUL'S ENERGY" by K.Tyrity

Together, we will explore and
experience our Spirits, and we
will feel them and sense them . . .
and then we will travel . . . to
journeys far beyond.

But first, let us deal with this
next item and use – The Color
Blue.

Now, the experience of Blue is a
Power . . . in its own. Its power
comes from the Sky . . . how
many skies I will not say.

But, the Color Blue comes from
the blue of the Universe.
Therefore, it is all-encompassing
– a stabilizing energy.

Its Power has its roots in your
own Consciousness.

Its Power can be used to heal
any organ in the body that is a
sac . ... gallbladder, kidney,
lungs, spleen.

Blue is a Power in Itself.

Its essence is the Number One . .
. the power of God in His Hand .
. . the Power of His Hand as the
Universe. This is something you
may not compute as of now, but
later I will explain to you what it
means.

Not every one of us has a
command of language the way
we should to express this. In
Spirit's communication, we talk
of nothing as you do in human
form. Our communication is,
what one might say, a little more
esoteric, perhaps a little more
involved. But you all have
knowledge of that.

So, BLUE is the color . . . ONE is the number.

Blue can stabilize your body. Blue is the symbol of wisdom . . . with the color Purple.

But, now we will talk about BLUE. Blue has the power to receive into it, all of your commitments as you project along in your perhaps otherwise dull life. What do I mean by that?

Pg. 7 – "TAPPING INTO YOUR SOUL'S ENERGY" by K.Tyrity

I mean that you should DESIRE
to receive the Blue into yourself ,
to receive the power to better
commit yourself to any project
or activity you may want to do
or complete – you should use the
Color Blue. To use this, place the
color Blue gently, very gently,
over both closed eyelids . . . two
dots of blue on the eyelids – then
place one dot of bright Blue in
the center of the forehead, and
one in the area of the throat.

We spoke before of the Diamond
of Blue on the throat in the
thyroid area.

Those three spots and the neck diamond in blue all lit up, with the Color Blue.

Now, wait for a few seconds and feel – Then, as for your commitment . . .
"I desire myself to commit to this book, or this project, or this whatever, -- activity that I am doing." Simply sit for the count of about a minute and a half there, enjoying and feeling it. Don't use a four and five year commitment with an hour long sit, but rather do it several times over the course of those intermittent projects and years.

As you sit then slowly get out of the pose, let the Blue Color slowly dissolve apart – until you are surrounded in just BLUE COLORS. Enjoy and then go ahead, get up, and go about your business as usual. There is no need to concentrate on your commitment except to see it in that light.

Blue has been the Color of Kings, has been the power of the Throne, and in its own way, it is the power that symbolizes the Truth of the Universe.

It is the power that goes far beyond . . . to Infinity, and forever!

And its communication in this Reality can be utilized in the fore-mentioned process.

Please understand, that, like any other process, you must take your time, and know that if you use it once a week for three or four weeks, it will help you in your necessary commitments to projects or undertakings, anything you do and want to complete with joy. As you go, if you want the help in your joy or commitment, use it once more. So, in other words, I am saying . . . don't rely on the process but rely on the courage it gives your Being.

Pg. 8 – "TAPPING INTO YOUR SOUL'S ENERGY" – K.Tyrity

And in your practice with The Colors Blue, be yourself. Don't concentrate on being pure, but only being as purely you and pure as you can be. Don't – whatever you do – try to be like "someone else." Just be yourself. And practice being as "good" as you can be to yourself and your own Truths.

(BREAK)

Every day that you exist in this Reality, it is an experience . . . leveling the different parts of your Being. Each and every one of you will eventually do the processes all or in part that have been given . . . maybe when you pick up the book again or another time altogether when the piece is given. There are many other messages in Kathy's work which are also available. These things you are reading may help you get along, and in the next few months, we would appreciate it if you would at least try them.

At the time of this writing of Kathy's, it is approaching Wintertime in the Far North . . . very inspirational. We will like to talk about the Christ and the Christ "Consciousness" with that time in the Winter. We will work on the acquisition and the feel of attaining the Christ Consciousness in everyone. We will want you to feel it, to sense it. And this part of your Nature will be exploring more and more of its energy – We don't just mean through November and December of this year, but on through February. Because some of the same energies will be present all winter long. Some of you are going along about the same, but some of you are looking for things yet to settle down. Oh, that is all right, because sometimes it takes one or two years, or three, to get to the situation where you will be more comfortable. So, be understanding of yourself as we work through this time and LEARN.

When we give you the processes to use in healing your body, it is very important that you understand, eventually, that there will come a book of these writings and you can order others. Just ask Kathy for the trance material and her thoughts.

Then, you can see what all the trance channelings are for, the colors and their uses, and the various classes which have been given. We are trying to bring you "Universal Truths" in these things which you could use.

Pg. 9 – "TAPPING INTO YOUR SOUL'S ENERGY" by K.Tyrity

Now, the only absolute truth here would be more of a guidance, a "divine" Guidance. Universal Truth is a wisdom and understanding about many different things. Universal Truths . . . as we go along . . . if you are willing to experience them, are available. There is no "stock answer" for anything. The only absolute here is the fact that you are a spiritual energy in a physical body. Then, beyond that, might I say : "Universal Truth . . . the Law of Cause and Effect . . . that is an absolute. That is the Truth." So . . . many people perhaps wonder – "When should I read a book? . . . Should I read that or should I read this?"

Well, sometimes you will be
learning something different
from that book – but that book
can be useful. However, it is
YOUR EXPERIENCE and how
you deal with it – THAT is your
Universal Truth. So
consequently, don't worry about
it. We are giving you about
everything you need to know
Universally. And . . . do you
know . . . we could pose this
question: Since there are more
than one Universe, what
Universal Truth would you like?

The one that applies here, or the
one that applies there?

So you see, it goes on and on.
And you should be considerate
of your personality here. Don't
wonder – boy I feel badly, I am
so far behind everyone . . .
Behind who? Who is ahead of
you? God? Who is ahead of you?
Me? I am not. I don't worry – I
just go along – I am learning just
like you, and I don't know who
is ahead of me or behind me.

Yes you see, I'm so busy wondering about what I am supposed to be doing . . . and that is what you should be doing, too . . . concentrating on yourself; don't worry about the others who like you are on a Spiritual Path as we. Don't worry about WHO is farther. And understand that since you are on this path, and all of you who are . . . it makes no matter – One piece of guidance that reaches you . . . or another and another . . . that is all that matters. You will understand the rest of it. But please, let us concentrate on the Universal answers.

You know, sometimes it is very hard for mankind – interesting work – man kind. . .very often man is not kind . . . but mankind to listen and understand. They want to find some far-reaching guidance . . . can it be possible and simple as all that? Yes. It is so. And so you see, what we give here in our
Pg. 10 – "TAPPING INTO YOUR SOUL'S ENERGY" By K.Tyrity

books in these pieces of paper will be extremely powerful. But of what usefulness is this power if you don't know how to act in any given situation with your own Nature? Power can be wasted. So, be willing to move along slowly so that you can expand yourself completely into YOUR OWN Universal Truth. And . . . if you have to sit there and scratch your head . . . that is all right. Then, we give it to you at a later time – at which time you will say, "Oh, yes, now I know exactly what she means."

I have this to share with you.
Each and every Personality that
incarnates in this world, does so
at his own choice, and therefore,
it knows What exactly to learn,
where it is going to be and how
it is going to get there.

Man-kind, because he is so kind
to himself, usually gets in the
way and says, "But wait a
minute, I don't want to do that! .
. . I want to do this over here."

And then he uses his willfulness and moves himself over here at work at this other. Then he experiences two or three other things . . . and that is fine. It is not incorrect, in fact, more than likely, it is probably perfect, because he needs to know how to let go of Willfulness and how else is he going to learn? So each and everyone of you who read these, has a need to learn these specific things which we give to you.

Now, I want you to picture your Consciousness . . . your brain inside . . . your brain. Where in the brain resides the Spiritual Energy? Well, we know that within the body is the spiritual energy . . . we tell you some of it is in the center of the chest. But we also know that some of this spiritual energy is within every pore and molecule and nerve and blood vessel of your body. However, within your Brain, as we have told you, is also the Spiritual Energy. And it resides at the base of the back of the skull in your body – in the back of the head is part of the center of your Spiritual Energy, as well as the other parts of your Being.

This may be a little confusing, but I am trying to show you that the brain is a part of Everything – it has its own Spiritual Center. And through this Spiritual Center, it receives Intuitive Messages.

Through this Intuitive Center in the Brain, it sends forth messages – to the emotional body.   (more of this text)
Pg. 11 "TAPPING INTO YOUR SOUL'S ENERGY"

Now, some of you may realize, that when you are very stressful and very highly emotional, you may have a tendency to get a headache . . . That is because the pressure is being built up in the Brain.

It is a normal reaction . . . everything rises to the top. The part of the Brain that holds the Spiritual Energy is full of guidance and intuition.

Many times, the brain gets in the way of the thought waves . . . the thought waves that are the brain . . . the mind center, the mind force. It comes this way – to the temple, around the head to the temple and it sends its message to the third eye (which is right in the middle . . . right between the bridge of the nose.) . . . It sends the messages right there. And if they are received properly . . . you hear them, or see them with your mind's eye if you are visual. It is the same inner guidance you need.

Tonight we will tell you the spiritual center, the brain's Medulla Oblongata . . . it helps you to receive your brain guidance – wisdom, knowledge, whatever it is that you need.

Now, sometimes it is very difficult to confuse that with the Mind Force . . . the mind force is different . . . that is, the Mind Force which says, "Oh yes, you can do it, who cares – do it anyway, or you are this or you are that." That is why, up until now, we have never brought it up. Because we don't want you to get into listening here . . . and thinking that you are listening to the right thing.

Whenever the body has a need
to receive past information
dealing with lifes, patterns or
habits, it comes from the
Spiritual Center of the Brain. If
you are aware enough . . . this
brain brings in forward
automatically . . . I show it
coming this way, but it comes
this way . . . So let's say this way,
it brings it right to the forefront –
Now, that doesn't mean you
have to become some
Enlightened Being; that simply
means you have to be in touch
with Your Self . . . here, this part
. . . because this deals with your
lifes . . . everything you have
been . . . all of your past patterns
. . . past habits . . . and beyond

that, your Emotion Nature.

Now, in some ways, one might think the Emotional Nature would be part of the chest, and it is to a degree. But by the time it is reaching here, it is totally vibrating . . . and it presses many triggers in the Being. When you feel pain here . . . in the back of this part of your head . . . you are undergoing a process of transformation from the Spiritual Center of your Brain.

It is extremely important that
you do not confuse this
information that we are giving
you. Because, again, as we go
along . . . don't worry about
"what do I do now with this
piece of news" . . . doesn't matter
. . . you don't have to go feeling
it . . . you don't have to go
wondering if you are hurting ..
. nothing.

Please believe me . . . I give to
you because I am anxious for
you to grow more. I'm trying to
help you to see the different
parts of your body . . . and why.
Someone might feel: "well, yes, I
feel here like that" . . . or
"sometimes I see back there."
Now, this is simply again, a little
food. Food for your Being.

As we go along, I will explain
more and more and more.

I have given you kind of a broad spectrum. But I will explain how the triggers work and WHERE they react and WHY they react. And sometimes, they even react inwardly . . . like action – you know . . . anger . . . inside anger . . . wanting to punch . . . wanting to be afraid . . . those reflexes come from the Spiritual Center of the Brain --- It is reminding one of the past events. It also holds the truth to dreams. But I don't want to go into that either, because then we get into a whole new spectrum . . . which we will do at some point in time.

Now, when you are particularly dealing with someone and you feel that this person is . . . a habit . . . say someone cropping up in your life all the time . . . . a "type" of personality – if you do use your Color Blue and put this color Blue in the back of your head, but at the base . . . not up here . . . at the base of your skull and surround . . . kind of over the ears up to the front of the forehead . . . just very lightly, color blue there . . . See the person you are having difficulty with. Ask to release that person . . . Ask to release to you any information that can be given on how to move through this situation . . . confidently, and

with more awareness, so that
you may rid yourself of the
problem completely. And then,
arise and move about . . . and so
then you shall receive that.

It occurs to me in these
channeling books, I give you so
many "processes" that it's tough
to find them and do them all. But
what with everybody every day
going through different things,
please do these and it will help
calm you and solve your
everyday problems.

So, sit in your "calm space," and do these every once in a while . . . oh, it's not a great problem you're working on maybe . . . but if you think about it when you are dealing with a specific personality or something in a situation, this will help you out. It will help you to "see." And, please, ask to see clearer – Say to yourself, "I desire to see more clearly." And desire to see what you can do to go through the situation you're in . . . and this will help you.

Guide yourself through the coming week by attuning your Nature to the needs of your Physical Body now. For the next seven days, why not take time to KNOW your body. See that it receives its proper nutrition and rest. And observe very carefully, HOW and what you use your body for. What you place on your body and in it . . . and whether you create a positive environment for your body to exist in. Use your awareness to see your body, with its faults as well as its strengths. Don't concern, simply be aware . . . if you feel a particular need of your body – then see that need, examine it and release it. Be aware of how you treat your body now and how you see yourself afterward. Above all, your thoughts and words are important to your Being.

Any thoughts or things that come near your Body during this time which seem negative or destructive, correct and say—"I choose rather to think loving thoughts of my body today."

Take steps necessary to initiate
CHANGE for your body . . .
even your thoughts are
contagious. So remember our
"joy" attitude to reap back the
love in everyday life. Have
loving thoughts for your special
Body then. Even if it is only a
thought, you might say it like, "I
desire . . . this, or I shall choose . .
. that." And observe your Body
carefully and your perspective
about your Body. Desire better
and choose better for it.

(spirit's space of silence here)

Now then, we ask you to please sit and place your feet flat on the floor . . . Visualize now in the center of your forehead, the color Purple . . . in the center of your throat, the color Blue . . . in the center of your chest, the color Green . . . in the abdomen area place the color Yellow . . .

We ask you to see at the top of your head, lying flat on top of your head, a circle of White. Feel that White enter your body . . . filling it from the head down to the toes . . . . . . feel the circles of color blending into the white . . .

Now, sit quietly for the count of
about twenty. And then we will
say Good Evening.

Beginning with this next lecture,
I would like to start
a creative visualization for you.

Concentrate on your forehead . .
. visualize in the center of your
forehead a diamond or circle of
Green . . . or a green pyramid
will do. See then from the left
and from the right a thin band of
Green . . . until it appears as
though you were wearing this
thin band of Green around your
head and in the center of your
forehead – till the diamond or
pyramid or circle of Green
appears…in the middle of your
forehead.

The Symbol of this process is
that it helps you recognize the
Spiritual Awareness in your own
Consciousness inside.

To help you prepare the way for your Consciousness to accept the coming lessons in these chapters, and in the books you may choose from Kathy's spiritual list . . . we are creating with these processes the energy necessary for you to receive your Wisdom and certain Knowledge.

These processes allow the Energy of the motivation to move more quickly into your Being, into the atmosphere you are in, into this Class. This then creates the Power, in 11 (a spiritual master number) in order for it to manifest properly at your Spiritual Center, your Spiritual Truth and its Greatest Wisdom.

We ask this evening that you be quiet and have patience with me. I am bringing to you two beings from Spirit who are invited, and sit quietly.

This first Being will instruct you on the processes which will be necessary for your "remembrance" of the facts in regard to your own previous lives – which, of course, reflect into this one…..particularly now when you are in the process of "letting go" and "letting god" with faith and wisdom. These things very often create blockages from one life to another.

If, in on and Life, you were – say
– very stubborn, and have
avoided any use of faith and
wisdom . . . Very often no matter
what you learned, you will be a
little "blocked" from that in this
life. You may find it difficult to
"let go" as you should be doing
with little things – And, you will
find it difficult to use Faith as
you do that. And difficult to
have Wisdom.

The wisdom may be there in this
Life for you, but there may be a
certain "unwillingness" to use it.

These things are like DOORS
that prevail upon your Nature –
and if you let go of
stubbornness, the final
achievement will be your seeing
the way to "let go" of the
willfulness.

So, these Doors seem to open,
these Doors include the color
processes and visualizations we
are going to give to you.

These process are not necessarily occult or meaning of the word which is study of the unconcrete or "unseen" things . . . unless you choose them to be . . . but it would have to be a truly significant space in which you would want to use them, like this Class. We would like to bring forth the past lives and all of their willfulness, all their "insecurity", all their "lack of stability." It brings forth into this Life . . . it brings that essence here and it takes it and transforms it, so that you may Create more of the Ability. Notice I said this: "You may create more of the ABILITY to see . . . to open those doors . . . to

keep them open, so that, this Life
may be one of your greatest
achievements in this planet.

And do not be concerned with
whether you shall or shall not
achieve. Simple Awareness is a
giant step, so don't use the word
"achieve" as a human does – as
you, a daughter or son of the
Universe – because it is not how
I do mean it. It is more
"achieve," meaning . . . one step
at a time.

Consequently, we would also like to share with you the reflection of other lives into this one . . . it will become a valuable tool in the next phase of your Life, after you do it, if you are paying attention. This is because each of you are going through situations in which you deal with one or several situations or people. One will be Mother or Father – another will be with worker or children. Again, worker meaning associate, your work environment, meaning your boss, meaning your secretary . . . whatever it may be. Any one of those, or perhaps all of them.

These are things that your Past Life create for you now with the necessity for you to come forth to greet and handle these . . . come forth that knowledge and confront it and accept it, and – open the DOORWAY, step through it and away from all that holds you back. That was lack of faith, stubbornness and willfulness.

The man from spirit is now here to bless you and create in you new Awareness . . . he has three aspects. He resonates with the letters B and N, and A – and the colors gold and purple. His vibration is from the Plane of Peaceful Endeavor. What would that plane of consciousness be in his vibration?

In certain Universes, there are certain Planes of Endeavor. Each Plane or dimension holds certain truths. Each Truth has a particular Avenue. I am condensing it since you do not live there and would not know about anyway. The Dove is the symbol of Peace on this plane . . . so he could very well appear to you as such.

Why would one who is from the Plane of Peaceful Endeavor create within you the need to see your Past Life? Or, the Past Life which most greatly influences this Life?

Because, when you let go of the past and all the "stoppages," then you will truly move through the DOORS that put in front of you your own Plane of Peaceful Endeavor.
Your Plane of Peaceful Endeavor . . . your peace and your path . . . your own Endeavor that is so important to you individually . . .will regain its truest Essence of your own spirituality. So, that means this: you will have reached that space in which you are one with your Being, complete with its Nature moving every so wonderfully and peacefully.

From the Plane of which this energy comes, for now, we give you the peaceful endeavor. I would not go around asking where it is as that will not apply. But in your own language, this is how you would understand it.

It does come from a dimension that cannot be reached my man's earthly consciousness – but in this man's truth and understanding, his Spirit and his Spiritual Power comes from . . . the essence that you all come from. Greater than that, however, is the Essence of his Truth. In this manner, you may find him to be a bit off balance . . . but that is primarily because he has never introduced himself in a verbal way . . . of communication way in this atmosphere. He hasn't been exposed to this planet . . . his primary purpose is to help attain peacefulness; therefore, he does better not manifesting in human for here in this Reality.

The process we shall begin now, will help you come closer to the Lifetime in which was created any situations that are now in this Life – any DOORS that are not yet open to you and respected.

Insight will be gained after reflection on your Person, after you do the process and reflection being your thoughts you may be having. Reflection whether it be your Truth in this Life, your Persona and Personality in this Life, your thoughts, and any other areas that you need to study to see beyond.

We shall work at uncovering
your life's reflections based on
the past Life which most directly
affects and enjoys this one. First,
let's learn the process. Then shall
we concentrate on an experience,
an experiment.

Each process or experiment will
have, it may appear, nothing to
do with the other; but each
process is a stepping stone to
uncovering the reflections as
they shall occur. Each of you
now need to become more
comfortable in your chair and
make yourselves aware of what
you are reading.

Your eyes are like windows – on both of your eyes – very softly as you close them, there lies a soft pink cloud. Just as though you had a cotton ball on each eyelid . . . 'tis soothing. As you feel this pink cloud, you sense its power . . . its love and the ability it has to see – even now as your eyes are closed, you can see your surroundings – the clothing you have on, the room, the place you are sitting, the sky outdoors.

Now . ... travel with me as these
clouds of pink are still upon
your lids . . . travel as though
you were driving your car and
taking yourself home. See the
outdoors; see yourself walking
to your front door. As you go in,
look around and see everything
there. Choose from your home a
favorite spot . . . a space where
you feel comfortable, warm and
loving.

See yourself now sit in that
space. As you do that, see what
is around you. Feel the warmth
and see even the smallest
particle of that space.

Now, see yourself standing outside of Your Self . . . watching you in your favorite space…self standing outside of yourself . . .watching you in your favorite space . . . Now become You again.

This space, this favorite space, is where we will discover our reflection.

Now, you will leave your home
again. See everything as you
walk out the door and as you
come here to where you are
sitting, remember your streets . .
. see now where you are, where
you are sitting, remember what
you are wearing. And now, you
are only aware of two clouds on
your eyelids, pink . . .and now,
let them go. You are now here in
your body, simply listening to
my voice.

In our travels to see our
reflections, we will look at the
mirror of Truth. This will help us
each to see the facets of our
Personality with more love and
compassion.

Each time we work in this
process you learn more. I would
prefer that you choose only to do
this process with this project.
The road to peace . . . the road to
travel in order to fulfill your
commitment through your
personal endeavor; there is never
a fear of not doing it – otherwise,
you would not be studying this
manual. But together we will
attain a level of understanding
that will help you to work with
your own peacefulness.

This will create for you a more
spiritual attunement to your
Life's purpose and work . . . even
if that work is your business; to
become closer associated with
your own personal endeavor,
and your environment can be
truly wonderful, harmonious
and fruitful.

As in all processes, we ask you
to be patient.

Each time you desire to study
these work manuals (the
channeled material of Kathy
Tyrity's and others') we will
review again some of the ways
to proceed with each project and
some of what has already been
given.

Do not be concerned or anxious.
What will be seen in only what
your reflection needs and no
more – what the reflection of the
Past Life needs to show you or
tell you . . . then you can learn
Why you are here in this Life
now and What you are and will
Become.

Each of you has expressed a
desire to "even out" – become
more "even." To be "detached,"
not to be "reactionary" to things
and people.

These "processes" or
experiments will also help for
this . . . to create peacefulness
through and in your own
environment, by NOT creating
any reactionary pattern.

Your skillfulness at discovering
what you are about . . . your
awareness for Truth . . . and
stability, your intuition or
psychic skill, whatever you call it
. . . all of these things will create
within you the motivation
necessary to receive the needed
Light of God within. The Light
of the World is upon this planet,
but it will take much before that
Light can be perfected
sufficiently to create
peacefulness.

It is, therefore, up to you to
create for your Self as much
peace as possible in order to
provide this planet with
Awareness it will need to receive
the benefits of the True Light
and Truth that shall be given in
the Future here. I will leave this
for now.

I accept all that you are. I ask
only of your consideration in
regard to your Nature and the
face that your Godliness shines,
in spite of any willfulness you
may still be carrying with you.

(Space of Silence, then)

We would ask you now to please take a short break . . . . .We ask you to gradually bring your consciousness into this room and to sit quietly while we do one more process with you, and then you can sit for the count of ten . . . and you will have your break.

The process begins as this: If you care to close your eyes, you may; it is not necessary that you shift your body. Repeat mentally after us – "We bring into our Being the need for Truth and Reflection. We seek our own Light and through that Light, we create our own Divine Knowledge.

We see within our Being in the
Center of our Consciousness,
which we know walks in the
Truth of the Christ Spirit. We
seek this Spirit, for it is our
Salvation, our Truth and our
Light. And we ask this Light to
bring us together with all of our
Selves, past lives and present.
And through this creation, we
will see our endeavor and seek
to trod the path firmly in the
directions of its truth for us on
this planet.

BREAK

Each chapter we will go over your betterment of your spiritual Self in order to produce the desired results. Often, do the band of green around your head, like between breaks or chapters. It is your choice to read these pages. And I am very intent on sharing the knowledge I have read and acquired. I desire that your participation be free and open. And through your participation, you will learn to experience a full spectrum of spiritual growth, spiritual understanding, and . . . much awareness of your Selves …. Mental, emotional, physical and the spiritual too. During this time, we may also experience our other Selves, the selves that existed or are existing in other dimensions, as has already been related to you.

We ask that you take time this
week to be aware, again, of your
physical body. The needs of your
physical body will change. It is
winter now as I am writing this
in a northern Ohio. The months
of February and March and
April are associated with the
color Green, the vibratory
number Three, and the letter C.
These times in the late Winter
are times for true understanding
of your Physical Nature – its
likes and dislikes, its habits and
patterns, its complete energy, or
lack of complete energy, desires
and needs, and the ability to
transform those things in your
Physical Body.

Every year, there is such a time
given when the awareness of the
physical Nature is greater than
at other times . . . this is these
three months of late Winter
where you are. During this time,
we wish you to have these
several Colors to use in regard to
the process of understanding
your Physical make-up.
You all have a need here, to
create more love for your
Physical Body.
This is something that has been
brought to your Awareness
before, but it still pays to have it
re-emphasized.

Physically, you are sometimes angry or frustrated or upset with your body, with its lacks or limitations, with its dislikes or likes, -- well, it is time to see your Physical Body as a loving instrument of growth and knowledge in this Universe. And that is Learning Foundation, your teaching ground. If immense you might have, say frustration with yourself. But have awareness of your own body's needs – personally, sexually, lovingly. . . whatever comes toward you, fend off with love or accept and find the love. So that, working hand in hand with this part of your Nature, you can express fully, accept it as

it is, and travel on its journey in
this Life.
You cannot assume you are
Spiritual and therefore separate
from the body, which you did
choose – by coming into this
world. And create it you did,
both inside and out.

So, now the sense of oneness one
must have with their spiritual
body comes from the Divine Self.

Divine Self means acceptance of that divinity within one's Nature. One may say, "I am God," One can say, "I accept I am Divine." One can say, "I accept I am spiritual" – but then one must realize that in accepting these things one must too, believe . . . In desiring to have one-ness with their Nature, they must always work at accepting it in order to feel and sense and know the one-ness is there. One-ness does not come automatically; it comes through careful consideration and understanding of the physical, the mental, the spiritual and the emotional. So, you cannot be out of sync; you must accept them

all in order to become one with
your Being.

One-ness with your Nature, your
Nature encompasses all parts of
your Selves, and your Nature is
everything you have ever been,
everything you shall ever be,
and everything that you are
now. It is, of course, only
important that you remember
the NOW; the other things will
take care of themselves.
Although, in some cases, it is
extremely beneficial to know
what you have been.

Some reflections will be given
now from the Being by the color
Purple of the third degree.

Hopefully I will not give you this wonderful insight into the Universe in which we exist and make you think there is some magical experience here for you, or . . . . ah, experience the Universe . . . I am using these terms because you associate with names, and so . . . I have no other way to express it to you. It does not matter to me that I see you one way and you have to see me in your way, but I will conform to whatever standard you have to see me in.

So, otherwise, I am not some magical person from St. Whoever or Universe Whatever. I am simply a Being . . . spiritual energy . . . purple three . . . purple three . . . that is simple.

Why am I purple three? Because I come from an area which the colors are all shades of purple. That means that my shade is number three . . . number three resonates with many tonal qualities in the Universe, your Universe of course. And I desire to share with you my extension of my Person-ality.

In our language, simple means of vibrations or the energy under which we exist. So, I exist under the number three. I deal closely with the human endeavor. As each one of you has been through difficulties in your life and acceptance, and I have been the one that has been providing the necessary energy to move through these times for many of my individuals on the planet where you are. Don't misunderstand; I don't run around all over the Universe helping every Soul that screams out, but I am my power, my Godly Self, my . . . . you might say . . . purple number three . . . does . . . it extends all over. But I am an energy, not so much as you would say, a "person."

Now, I would like to begin to give you the key to help your acceptance of "WHAT IS."

I know each one of you has dealt with WHAT IS and mostly you can deal with it and have accepted that. But some will have doubts about their future, about their present, about their knowledge, about their time and about how far are they?

Dealing with respect is the first key. What is dealing with Respect like? If you are dealing with your Self and you are exhausting your Self through committing your Self to energy or participations in events that seem negative or destructive, then you are holding no respect. Respect your Nature. Respect your needs. Respect your love. Respect your Person. Respect your growth. Respect your body. Respect your Personality. Respect cannot just be used. I respect my Self because I am loving and kind . . . and then you turn around and you say, "I don't deserve this," or you turn around and you do something that you know is going to affect you emotionally . . . or you turn around and your body says you are tired, but you say, "I must continue, I NEED to do it." Then why is it you feel you have respected yourself; you have respected a part of your-self, but not all of your Self.

Now, it is sufficient to say that respect is on many different levels. Therefore, we must learn each one, in order to totally respect ourselves. You can't just respect one aspect and forget the rest. You must work at respecting.

It is how to attain one-ness
through acceptance and
emotional respect. How can you
accept what you don't respect?

You may say to yourself, "I am
tired, but I need to go on.. .."
then you are certainly not
accepting, because if you did
accept you would also have to
say, "I accept that I am tired, so I
must listen to my body and
rest."

So you see, when you know the circumstance called for action, you cannot just accept and then let it go – you must complete the action in order for the acceptance to be utilized properly. Otherwise, you are just mouthing words. You are saying, "Yes, I accept."

Of course, there are circumstances in which you must accept and move on . . . those are obvious. And if you look at them, you will see that they are obvious. But to accept and then turn around and pay no heed to acceptance and respect . . . you are not creating anything. Above all, you are certainly not creating respect . . . or acceptance. So you are scurrying around thinking that you are doing things good . . . so remember. And, again we are not here to badger, but we are here as the group – to instruct you on the other facets of these responsibilities to your Self that you have chosen on this Earth.

This "awareness" that you seek,
awareness of Self, knowledge
and understanding, love and
expression of your Christ Light .
. . this will come forth. Then, if
you are going to utilize the Light
properly, fully and completely,
you must learn through the
processes that you are being
given . . . that means – respect,
acceptance . . . acceptance . . .
respect.

At the same time, accept
gratefully . . . respect . . . think
about that!

Is it easy for you to respect your Self, but not to allow others to do the same? Do you allow others to respect your self? Or do you allow others to create disrespect? If so, you are still not making the respect for your Self.

As you go along, we will continually remind you of the different facets of self respect and acceptance. Because you desire what you are here for. . . . . spiritual one-ness with your Self, and that is what you shall receive. But you must work to acquire it.

BREAK

We will now talk about the
manifestation of the Christ Light
. . . the manifestation of Christ
Consciousness . . . the
manifestation of Truth . .. its
creations.

It is impossible to express the
availability each of you has to
feel and sense your one-ness
with the Christ Spirit.

. . . it is your Essence and your
spiritual energy that creation of
the Christ Consciousness to
become attained.

It is the combination of all Souls
and all Beings in whom resides
the Light . . . the combination of
all those Beings create spiritual
power necessary to bring forth
the spiritual power of the
Universe.

It is the complete Essence of
those Beings, that is created here,
on this Earth – the desire for
more under-standing, more
respect, more love and more
compassion.

In your world, there will be events that will create disappointments, discouragements. But the necessity to harbor in each one's Being the compassion and love of the Spirit in order to prepare this Universe for the energy of its truest compassionate Spirit . . . it is necessary for the aliveness of every individual that walks the Earth.

Pain and suffering are not in the scheme of God's work, but Life is a trial and error. Mistakes will be made.. . . . but no judgments, but rather acceptance of what is.

To create one-ness of the Spirit, one-ness of one's Truth and Spiritual Direction, one must see without the blinders of the atmosphere and this Planet's energy . . . but rather to share of their spiritual Truth and through love and understanding. The nature of your Being is respect, the Essence of your Being is Truth. And through the effort of many, it will be discovered again that the simple word LOVE is all the compassion that is necessary to overcome difficulties.

Your Being has placed itself in a Generation in which Truth and Understanding are its grandest demands.

The spiritual awareness of your own person has created the need for more continuity between man and man, or woman and man, or woman and woman. You cannot begin to know of other Universes until you begin to LIVE in your own. You cannot choose to be here and not experience your Life. Your nature is God. Your Essence is Christ Consciousness. And throughout your Life, if you choose to discover your spiritual endeavor, you will always put your Self at home within your own Temple of Truth.

Here we give you ideas and concepts. Here we give you creativity and questions. Here we show you how to learn and know. But you are the ultimate test of all that is given in this series of teaching in these books.

We do know that man and
woman have a desire to succeed
in their own personal
knowledge, so then we give you
a gift . . . the awareness of Truth
within your own Nature which
is sufficient to provide you
energy to thousands of people.
The power of your own Spirit
and its loving Self, learning and
growing and experiencing is
sufficient to continue the
evolutionary process of this
planet.

Step forth into your own space
and know that the reflection of
that space will give you what
you need. Seek – not in far away
places, but rather, seek in your
own Home within.

The Christ Consciousness that
each of you seek to attain is
within reach, but often is
ignored through lack of
commitment to one's Self. So,
continue to place your feet
firmly, one after the other, to be
continually aware of the lessons
you are learning, the experiences
that you are involved in and
even the criticisms from others
in the world.

See beyond those things – to a space deep within yourself, to attain the freedom of Spirit, your Spirit, and its desire to see its own Truth.

And now we would like to do another "process." This process is called the desire to see Truth honestly and completely, but you may associate it with a letter and a number. It is associated with the number 8 and the letter E . . . We ask that you concentrate now on this process we are about to give you.

It is within your complete
Essence that you can attain a
certain amount of stability in
order to seek Truth, in order to
see your Truth, in order to
understand Truth.

By becoming aware of the number 8 and the letter E, its process can begin, if you practice. It is not to be used in a competitive or forceful manner, however. If you are working with a problem, or if you need to know or understand a situation or person you are having trouble with, as though perhaps you are not seeing it correctly – then, use this process definitely. Again, mention the words with the number and the letter, is enough to bring your awareness into the perspective of the process. So, if you can practice for a few times, become familiar with it, and then one day you can mention the number and the letter and it will

come right to you – the energy to
solve the problem.

So, the process is this, if you care
to join in.

The visualization is: in the center of your chest, you are to see a five-pointed star, it is like shining rays, beams of light coming out, all around the star. These beams are white light. The center of the star is pink and the light beams are white. As you look, it appears as the star and the beams of light are shining outward from your chest to infinity. Now sit for a few moments. Ask yourself the questions now . . . "I desire to see the truth about such and such and to deal with it accurately. Visualize the five-pointed star with the beams of light, see it or sense it, or feel it, or simply be aware of it going into infinity . . .

shining out from the center of
your chest. After a certain time,
then let it go.

If there is something you need to think about during that time, this will be the time to think about it. Roll it over in your mind. Maybe you don't get a decision right away, but just observe it; see the problem, sense the problem, talk about the problem to your-self, and then let go of the light and the question. Get up and go about your business. If you desire to receive an answer still, at that point you may sit for a few moments and then see it may come. Don't be too concerned, but look for the answer. It will be shown.

And now we will take a short
break.

BREAK.

In your spiritual Growth, there
always comes a time in your life
in which you are made more
aware of the possibilities that
exist in your immediate
environment, in your personal
involvement, in your
associations with other people.
Spiritually, you always attune
yourself to the highest and best
which is for your benefit.

When one attunes themselves
more completely in one-ness
with their spiritual Being, their
Spiritual Center, this then puts
you in direct relationship with
your Spiritual Path . . . therefore
creating more possibilities . . . .
therefore creating one-ness with
all that is and all that shall be.

Your Spiritual Power, and its ability to help you in your Spiritual Growth, can only be accentuated by creating the one-ness with your Self. Therefore, that means that harmony and love, acceptance and respect, understanding and compassion for your Being . . . . each and every time you use these, you create more one-ness, more power, more spiritual energy and more awareness of your personal Spiritual Truth.

Each and every one of you are different, and yet sometimes some are similar or some are the same . . . these are only similarities, tendencies, habits, essentially, of course your Essence is all God, all encompassing and all Truth.

Understanding that you are one
with each and every Being puts
you into the perspective of
accepting each and every Being.
Treat each and every Being as
though they were your brother
or sister. This does not mean that
you must always turn the other
cheek, but only to respect their
dignity and Divine Self, maybe if
you should, move on . . . To
accept the divineness to their
nature, but not choose to
participate in their environment
is essential to your Being, if that
is your task. The Essence of each
individual that walks the Earth
is the same, but beyond that,
their lessons and experiences are
very different.

Each of you travels through Life with particular Souls in which you need to experience their energies and their person, their environment and their habits and patterns. Some are attached only to the spiritual vibration of one another; others are attached in many different ways . . . mental Self, emotional Self, physical Self. Each of your friends has a particular avenue which they proceed on in their relationship with you. This is their training ground, their learning, their lesson, their Truth, if, of course, they choose to see it in that manner. None of you are together for any particular karmic reason, but

mainly to experience again, the
one-ness that you shared in
other lives with truth and spirit.

Many times people are brought
together to experience again,
great truths and knowledge . . .
to again create from a past
energy a power that will carry
each individual off into their
own direction most completely
and fully.

If you are in this original lecture,
each of you has joined together
with another, whether it be here
or elsewhere, to create a spiritual
vibration. Each time you shared
in this class you create a spiritual
vibration. The spiritual vibration
then sends out from this group
its energy; that energy seeks out
those who need Truth. In its own
power, it helps to manifest truth
in those who are also seekers . . .
beyond those who share this
material among themselves and
did in the class. The vibration of
energy you are creating is then
spread out through those with
whom you have experienced
other lives in the past, those
whom you have a karmic cause,

those who are just attuned to your energy, and those who have a Spiritual connection. Everything you learn from this book, every energy you create with this knowledge, every process you use with this work, benefits not only you but those with whom you continually come in contact with, or have been in contact with, as well as your other Selves, in other dimensions. This is HOW you share what you are learning without ever speaking a word.

You Spiritual Energy in this participation creates another power. This power is above and beyond the human existence. When you are studying with us, you choose to be responsible for your Being. When you "love" your Being this way, you then create in your Spiritual Energy a real Power. All our participation in these groups and our spiritual Beings create more power. That power, then attunes itself to the spiritual evolution of this planet. Hurray!

Every being who has a desire to spiritually attune themselves to their own Spirit . . . to their own spiritual Being . . . creates a power that is then given in a shared way, to the spiritual experience of this planet. So that, each and every time you are, one might say, moving in your chosen Spiritual Endeavor like this, you add to the Spiritual Evolution and process and progress of the planet as a whole.

This study notes is how life evolves. This is sometimes how some of our Love comes into being. This is how individuals learn, not necessarily through conscious awareness, but through spiritual spontaneity and spiritual understanding . . . inner subconscious experience. It is also important to understand that your spiritual energy has a commitment to its other Selves. Other Selves, meaning that parts of its Nature that are experiencing in other dimensions . . . that commitment extends beyond time and space. Everything you learn here is transferred to an energy that is given, through like electromagnetic fields to your other parts of your Being.

At the same time, everything that you learn in such a Spiritual manual, over and above, in other words from your daily ritual, is always Spiritual, yes, but some can be negative and some can be positive . . . these are all given to your spiritual Self, for Greater Soul. There is it stored for future reference, for future awareness.
THE PURPOSE OF ONE'S LIFE

No one person can magnify
what the meaning of their Being
is, sufficiently to make one
aware of the totality of their
existence in the Universe. The
greatness of your Being cannot
be experienced totally until you
leave this earth and then you are
aware of the expanse and
limitless power that is yours.
And at that point, the minor
attachments to this planet
become almost non-existent.

The freedom of your awareness,
the choice to move on to greater
things . . . this awareness was all
within your being, within every
Being. The truth of one's Nature
is always closest to one's Inner
Self at the moment of death.

The transition into another
awareness is simple. And one
does not necessarily have to be
concerned with what was – in
fact it may not matter anymore.
The sense of completion of one's
Life comes from knowing the
greatness that will follow! For,
the next step that takes place,
takes them into another
dimension that is far greater
than where they were. The
transition from one Life to
another Life is simple. And one
need never think of one's past
until the absorbtion . . . through
Self awareness and one's next
experience.

Essentially, the extension of
one's life into space is like
stepping off a cliff and then
being taken without the
cumbersome feeling of one's
body. The Essence of all spirit is
free and its greatest satisfaction
comes from the moment of
truthfulness of its Essence . . .
and life doesn't really matter
which has already been said and
done.

BREAK

This year is a year of depth. This year we choose to give you items to think about which will be useful for some time to come. We will be in the process of fine-tuning, smoothing out . . . giving you a greater understanding of these tid bits of information. You are learning to take more responsibility for your spiritual energy. You ARE the creator, you must choose to allow what you create to manifest. No longer can you come to study time and simply be an observer, you must be a participant in the energy . . . not just a pleasant reader. This is not for our benefit as much as it is for your benefit.

For now, for you to be able to receive unto your Being, Truth and the highest and best quality of Truth, you should prepare somewhat. Be aware of the inner saying, "I am God." God Within. And with that saying, you should go deeper and further as we move along.

We shall now make you aware….that you can be a stream of light in the darkness ahead . . . the need of Truth . . . the darkness of Beings in search of the greater Reality.

Hold on to your Human Self, because it is your partner in this relationship between your Spirit, this earth and your Human Self. Do not work against your partner but rather WITH your partner.

In the coming chapters, see if your desire to achieve more spiritual growth . . . along with the care and awareness of Self – will choose the ride or somewhat to escape here and there -- Or, does it choose the Human experience to learn its own Spiritual Truth through its experience.

BREAK

Each of you has acquired a certain amount of stability through your Growth. Pay particular attention this coming week to your work relationships. Those people you interact with during your work relationships will begin to show you an emotional awareness regarding your Nature. Those of you who are not in work relationships should observe the person that is the closest to you. This energy is very similar. You are to look at your emotions in regard to your work associates.

THE PROCESS OF 'LETTING GO' AND LETTING GOD HELP

The process of letting go, the
need to bring one's Self into a
state of willingness to let go and
let god . . . this letting go is most
difficult, as this a Universe of
such trials.

The process of letting go is associated with the color Purple and the number 9, and the letter S. The desire to forgive through the process of letting go, the desire to be let go of attachments, the desire to let go of what does not belong to one's Nature, the desire to let go of concern, the desire to let go of anxiety . . . all these things must be worked through. Please understand, if you are anxious and you need to work through the anxiety first, then using 'letting go' will not work at first. You first must work through the anxiety and know that you are resolving it, but still are faced with the problem of through feeling it – then you may use the letting go process we shall give you soon.

Put yourself in a beautiful imaginary Light of Purple Rays – totally surrounding your body – and feel it radiating from your body . . . inside and out, the beautiful Color Purple.

As you sit within this Color Purple, feel as though the Color becomes endless . . . you are surrounded everywhere with the Color Purple.

Bring your awareness then into the center of your chest, and see there a golden Circle of Light . . . this golden Circle of Light becomes a stream of Light, and it, too, becomes endless.

What you desire to 'let go' of, at this time, mention in mentally or aloud, and see the picture visually if you can. Now, then, at this time – Ask your Being to work to move into and through the simple process of 'letting go' of it. When you have let go. God 26 begins, but only after it has risen up to Him/Her God. There is more to this process, but that is sufficient for you to understand how it works.

Each of you will be dealing more these days with your emotional Self. This is not to create concern with your Nature, but to make you aware of the part of your Being that is now being expressed.

Spiritually, your association with your emotional Self teaches you about your Love, your Childishness, and your emotional Control.

See it in your work. See it in the person who is closest to you. It is a reflection that will teach you much about your own Nature.

We are now going to bring the classwork to a close for a pause. We shall close with a simple process that will be for your own Being, if you do it, as well as for those who are in need, so to say.

In the center of your chest, see the pulsating White Light . . . it is in your spiritual center . . . it becomes magnified with love and light . . . and see it now go into the center of the room. There it resides . . . a ball, a circle of white golden light . . . into the circle you may place anyone you choose . . . you may see their face, their Being, a picture of him or her, their name on a piece of paper, whatever choice you make here. Place them in that Light . . . see this light envelop their Being, with love and kindness, with acceptance and spiritual Truth. See this light penetrate their whole Nature.

Now, let that person go their way, and each one who has placed their light in the Center . . . now see that Light reach into your Being . . . completely envelop your body and soul . . . Feel now, your Center's one-ness with your Spiritual Power.

May your coming week be peaceful and kind. May you love your Self, and above all, may you be observant of your own Nature.

Emotions can be extremely controlling. Therefore, know that emotionally it is not fair to your Self to control your Self or to use your emotions in those ways, manipulating out of love or caring. Your emotions are a reflection of anger and frustration that has developed through past actions or even past habits, past circumstances actually. Do not be afraid of your emotions . . . but make sure that are stable as well as useful.

Please remain seated for several moments, then read on.

BREAK.

Now, if you would, please, just
inhale and exhale . . . inhale
through your nose and exhale
through your mouth . . . . just to
let go of whatever energy or
energies you might have
participated with during the day
. . . also to bring your Being into
Balance. Let go of anything that
may have affected you during
the day . . . . personal problems
or otherwise -- . . .

We ask you now to visualize in the center of your chest . . . a circle of pink. Sitting inside the circle of pink is a golden cross. Simply see it . . . placing it gently on your chest . . . be aware of the spiritual energy that resides within your Being. And as you see that spiritual energy from a beam of Light that flows into the center of the room. Place in the Light any person you feel can be helped mentally, emotionally, physically or spiritually. See them in the center of the circle of golden white Light.

And now if you will, repeat after me, mentally.. "We ask that all Beings receive unto themselves, the Light of Illumination, healing and conscious awareness of their own Spiritual strength and energy. And that they bring to themselves a feeling of complete at-one-ness with their own spiritual center . . .

And now, release them . . . let go of their names, vision of their faces and also let the Light go . . . and just let them disappear.

Whenever you are alone and you choose to be aware of the need of other people . . . of the need to bring guidance and illumination to their consciousness, you may do this same process . . . sending the Light from the center of your chest to the middle of the room and placing the Being in that Light will be more than sufficient to help them acquire a certain amount of illumination and healing. The process of this energy is almost instantly attuned to their spiritual Nature. The power of thought goes extremely quickly. If you are working with concentrating on another Being and allowing them to heal themselves of illness, that energy takes a little while longer. But if it is only to illuminate their consciousness, that they gain their own spiritual strength, and that they feel your lovingness and your Truth, then that is almost instant, almost instantaneously. And every time, of course, your Being chooses to do that . . . what you do to your own Nature, is create more of a stabilizing effect, too, not only within your own Being, but with your own Spiritual Energy.

The formation of your spiritual energy is, again, a topic in this manual.

Even though we have give you
bits and pieces on the formation
of your Spiritual power and how
this power takes its own
presence in your life, we know
still, full well, that it is a matter
of transition for your spiritual
power to take its rightful place in
this Universe – and to be able to
utilize that spiritual power to its
utmost capabilities.

When you are young, when you are little, your formation of spiritual power is still a part of your Nature . . . as we have explained before . . . separate from your body. It resides outside of your body, but connected to the center of your Being. This power . . . the more you adhere to your spiritual energy, becomes fed by the spiritual energy. As you become grown and you pay more attention to your Nature, the spiritual power develops its own foundation, from what you have created before; before you came into this lifetime even.

So, again, this sounds all very technical, but at the end of this work, you should be to understand these and many other secretly held truths of the Universe with you. But it will be necessary to understand these things in their own form . . . so that they may be given in different stages; different books of mine, all available . . . thereby creating a new awareness of your Being each and every time that you study.

We will now look at the power of transformation.

The reason we are giving you this now is to make sure of the transitionary nature of your Personality at this present time.

Everything as it now appears will be changed, even those things . . . one might say . . . that have created or are tinadequacies in your Nature. . . . . those things that are erratic behavior . . . fluctuations of your energy . . . . attitudes . . . conflicting people . . . feelings of 'out of sync' . . . . the lack of your being on a solid foundation. All of these things are part of your transition power.

When the transition is complete, then again, use the color green which will help you to deal more completely with your Spiritual Power in its transformational process. It is winter here now and by spring we'll have it done . . . so work steady at this for several months, especially in the Winter months . . . for the transformational process . . . the realization of what has taken place in the past . . . the accommodation of your own Spiritual energy, in an uplifting way, in accordance with your Personal Being.

So, there are many things here,
which must be taken into
consideration . . . it is not just the
Earth changes, or the weather,
nor people's problems, nor your
neighbor's attitude . . it is all
having to do with your own
spirituality.

The dormant time of winter is good for spiritual changes while the earth too is dormant and awaits a new Springtime. It is a time of achieving Christ Consciousness . . . of pulling into your Personality the awareness of your own Spiritual Self . . . not just intellectually but intuitively. . . . inwardly, wholly, completely. So that, when it fills ever pore and essence of your Being, you will again realize that its most powerful energy is transformation throughout this time of life.

And throughout all of your life
there is more transformation, so
you see, the process does not
stop . . . it is a continuation of
your evolution on this Planet . . .
a continuation of your spiritual
energy for centuries and lives
and lives and lives.

What you have chosen to do in this Life is only a part of what you will do, 'tis only a part of what you are doing now . . . part of you will do . . . What you will do later on is MORE than you are doing now. And this is not just jobs, work environment . . . it is HOW TO EVOLVE IN THIS REALITY, so that you can be the best, transform the most, cleanse that Being to the utmost, so that when you complete this certain Life, it will be full of experience, joy, harmony and one-ness with your own Spiritual energy . . . thereby creating for yourself a most positive vibration unto which you exist in your next Life whether it be on this planet or another; be it another reality or simply an expression of your own Spirituality.

<u>These things are important to your Nature.</u>

And every year while Winter sleeps, you have the power to give yourself more ability to also transform yourself. And as you can or will see over the years, this and Kathy's other works give you more and more information to study. This manual seems in depth…a little more, one might say . . . meat to the subject. So it may sound confusing, but, believe me, sooner or later you will know of what I speak.

It is important to recognize that the time, winter is so important. This time of year is a spiritually attuned essence, the reason being, of course, the Christ-mas and Christ Consciousness is stronger at this time and seems so spirit filled.

Also, during your Lifetime . . .
the time you have chosen in
which to take your own spiritual
direction, is upon you. You may
have thought that your spiritual
direction was, up until now,
what you were doing, but it is
not. As you read these pages
prepare for guidance and more
intuition, which is a nice way to
deal with lifestreams, allow for
more spiritual consciousness.
Not only to change your planet,
but to change internally and
externally by your nice
countenance. Everything that we
give you is to help the molecules
in your very body . . . endure,
accept, be faithful, inside and
out.

When we say to you that the power of transformation is upon you, then you will know what that means to your Being. You will know that is the time to be kind to Being, to be respectful, to not over-indulge. Not over-eat or over- drink. This means even . . . just food in general. But to exercise more, and work and rest . . . it is not a time for OVER anything stressful. It is a time for balance, kindness and respect to the spiritual body.

In its own essence, your spiritual power and the formulation of that power was created so that you may have the utmost in abilities during the time of transformation.

So, for the most part, each and
every year you practice
awareness and understanding of
yourself . . . you recognize you
trust your faith, you accept all
these things . . . add to the power
of your spiritual center, thereby
creating more attunement to
your own spiritual foundation.
And this is where the power of
Christ lies . . . this is where it will
take you to your final
destination of your spiritual
journey with your Self . . . not
with your neighbor, not with
your husband, nor even your
work, but with your Self. You
see, each and every one of you
who have chosen to study this
material do so because you need

that, but beyond that . . . because your spiritual path has brought you to this realm, this will help you to move on further in your destination, even if this is the only book you read of this nature. It still will help you activate within you the power of your spiritual Being.

During this period of transformation, which as we say now is beginning Winter in Ohio, this is the time for positive thinking.

During this period of transformation, which as we say is thinking.

Now, one might think "I always think positive – I don't do anything else but!"

Well, I suggest this . . . look at your Nature, look at your past few weeks and ask yourself, if every utterance from your mouth, every thought has been positive . . . or has it been a little bit the other way? Was it a little – one might say – putting your Self down, has it been a little anxious, has it been not satisfied or fulfilled with your life? That is not positive!

Transformation means you must attempt to be balanced . . . in spite of anything or all the rest of it. You must let go of, you must be willing to give up some things you overindulge in . . . you must be willing to see yourself as a human Being in a physical reality with a spiritual energy. And you must be willing to accept all parts of your humanness, and therefore also your aches and pains, your little "negatives," your thoughts must be accepted, but they must be let go of and not focused upon. So, don't allow the words or the thoughts to get carried away. You must learn to let go and believe.

Transformation is also the time for faith . . . in spite of all the conflicts . . . in spite of all situations that may appear to be negative . . . that may even appear to be . . . inconsistent with your life or your Nature . . . that is the time to let go of it and say, "I know and I believe that this will soon be over. I accept what is, but I have faith that it will change."

I cannot begin to tell you how important it is to use faith and the power and process of transition.

Now, the power of transition must also be utilized with the power of faith, because transformation is a non-seeing event. It is a sensing, an intuitive knowingness, and it is using the power that you have now attained to transform those attitudes and ideas and even resentments that you might have of the past . . . People, situations, events . . . thinking of what you don't have as opposed to what you do have, thinking of your lacks or so you think . . . of the words in general and of your attitude towards it.

This power of transformation
can lift the level of your own
awareness, so that you can let go
of all that. No longer will you
have to feel intimidated by other
people or situations or events,
but rather, you can transform
this energy into a loving
compassion of understanding
and personal pleasure through
joyful association of Being,
sharing with one another . . .
theirs and your own loving
spiritual energies.

Like we said, in Christmas time and through these couple few months surrounding December 25, is when the power of our own personal transformation is the strongest. And nowadays even more so. It is so strong lately because things are speeding up. They are accelerating . . . you cannot any longer play make-believe because then you couldn't pay attention. In this you must pay attention. It is too easy to fall into old habits, and it is too easy not to listen to the voice that calls your own home within . . . your Personality and the transformation of that Personality is at hand.

So we ask you to study with
others and seek out more of
these kinds of books and reading
materials to help you to keep a
balance as you move through
your personal Nature through
transformation times of year . . .
so that during the period of
transformation, during this
transformation event, you can
work the utmost with your
physical Being and emotional
and spiritual and mental being.
And we do not give them just for
your enjoyment; we give them
for your use and for your
benefit.

The other key is this: to make
sure that, once a day, if you can,
please spend a few quiet
moments with your Self . . . to
attune yourself to your energy,
to remind your Being that you
are NOT this body, that you are
NOT this mind, that you are
NOT of this world or this
problem or aggravation, that you
are SOLID inside, that you are
REAL and – that Reality is your
own Inner Being in its Spiritual
Consciousness.

Through that endeavor, you will
begin to see a sense of stableness,
a sense of solidity – and that
solidity will carry you through
any erratic nature of transition . .
. And also will give you the
awareness through meditation
times of the power of your own
transformations.

The power of Transformation, in its own essence is good; it is the power of your own spiritual energy to utilize transformation, its spiritual center and the Power that resides in the Universe. These three things combined to make the Power of your own Transformation an experience that your Being needs and loves to have . . . an experience that you desire to have and such a one that would help your Being "climb" over, one might say, any circumstance or situation past or present that's the problem. The three powers of your Being work together to teach you, your Inner Nature, and your Outer Nature the presences of your inner

Spiritual energy. Thereby,
creating inwardly and
outwardly, a sense of
knowingness; creating more
power to your intuition, more
presence of your personal
awareness and to change those
things that need to get changed –
I mean those parts of your
personality.

Transformation is not only to
clean up what has taken place –
whether it be way past or
immediately past, but also to
help the physical and emotional
Nature to transform its energy . .
. the molecules, the atoms . . .
and even the organs of the body.

These things, too, take the presence in the transformation of energy . . . What takes place to those in a power of transformation?

That is when, if they desire a certain amount of awareness and love, of understanding toward their Being, that is when that rises, that is when they are given insight into their Personality . . . that is when they see their willfulness, their selfishness, their lack of respect for their Being, their lack of compassion and understanding. It confronts them immediately and then the spiritual energy within helps them to see the need to change their Being. Of course, that being their choice, whether they do so or not.

So, the power of Transformation works through everyone's life, but in yours now in particular, you will finally have the chance to rid yourself of the Past. Those of you who are dealing with the opposite sex, for instance, should have a clearer insight, decisiveness . . . strength and courage to see clearly. Those of you who are dealing with their physical body will see the need to make certain changes, through respect of your Nature and your temper. Those of you who are dealing with family . . . mother or father . . . will see clearly how to achieve acceptance, how to deal with the personalities, their energy . . . sometimes their

negativitsm. And those of you
who have had difficulty with the
father will see in which ways to
work your personality in regard
to that parent. And how, in turn,
the parent can see you as a
viable, successful individual and
respect your Being.

This power is ever-present in Nature. This is the time now to rid one's Self of past habits . . . and I don't mean small idiosyncrasies that pop up every once in a while . . . I mean even in some cases . . . most of you could tap into other lives in which you had such habits as this. So also habits, also father and mother, father and physical being . . . this is the key to today. This is the key to this period of transformation.

There is one more that is also very important . . . and it is your relationship, your perspective and perception . . . of what your spiritual energy means to yourself. How you perceive your spiritual being. How you desire to express that Being. And if you pay close attention during these winter months . . . you will see insight into your own Spiritual Power.

If you take the time to ask yourself: "How and what do I think of my Being and its expression of spirituality? How do I relate to it?" And, "What is it I desire to do with it at this time?" Well, do that, and then while you don't look for an answer for it for the rest of your life . . . but at this time only. Then so be it. How do you perceive these things to be? Where has your attention been in regard to your spiritual growth? And how can you connect even more with this enhancement of your Spiritual Power? Answers should be forthcoming. This is the Transition stage now . . . leading the way to

transformation that will give you
insight to your questioning
Being.

So you see . . . . it will be worth it
to move through transition.
Accept, and believe . . . that
transformation will take its
rightful place in your Nature –
and, with your help and your
awareness and your desire to be
in touch with your Inner Being . .
. it will complete its cycle in this
season.

Most of you are seeking. Most of you have a need to connect, or to know, or to feel a sense of satisfaction . . . to sense your intuition or 'psychic' self . . . your spirituality . . your Inner Self. And so . . . listen . . . observe . . . be aware . . . and you shall hear it and you shall have it.

And, each of you who has
worked so intensely . . . with
your Being . . . sometimes too
intensely . . . sometimes not
enough . . . But that is not a
problem. 'Tis simply in your
experience now, but I guarantee
you that at some point in time,
whether it be soon or a couple
three-four years, you certainly
will attain it. And, everything
now can be used forever. This is
not just given to you for this time
. . . from these moments on, you
will find the power of
Transformation to be extremely
valuable in your life and lives.

When you formulated your spiritual Power, when you gave it its presence in this Reality, you also gave it permission to help achieve a balance within your Nature. Otherwise, you would never have turned within. And so, no matter what space you are in presently, know it by simply needing to know the Inner Being, by simply desiring to change; and you have given and activated the permission in the spiritual Power to help the level of understanding through your spiritual energy. So, you see, you are not alone. You created the body, you created the Personality, and you created the attitudes, your created also the way out of them. It is not some figment of your imagination or God's miracle, it is your OWN miracle . . . you created that.

It came from the power of Godliness, yes . . . but you created it. You gave it power from your Being and it to your Being. You know its strength. So, the formulation of your Spiritual Power was created by your Self . . . to save the Personality . . . to help this poor Being, as you call it. I don't see it as a poor Being . . . YOU may see it as a poor Being. If you could see it as I could see it, you would realize a totally different perspective of yourself.

So, you created for yourself a
safety valve. All it takes is . . . .
attunement, acceptance,
understanding, balance – and
this then feeds the furnace with
the power of its own Christ
Consciousness – and there is
power in the Christ
Consciousness . . . you're not
without it . . . You from where to
receive it . . . because if you have
not attained it . . . . in a form here
. . . it is part of this. So . . . here is
the key . . . another key to help
you recognize . . . your Being.

To help you see . . . the Truth of its own Self. And above all, all the prayers that you have been asking for help and guidance are right here next to you . . . so you don't have to call long distance . . . it is part of your very Nature. All you need to do is express to your own Being . . . "I believe within me resides my spiritual Power that is not attached to this world, but only for the time being, to my physical body. It is where I learn; it is how I grow, but it is not all I am."

Now, let us take a few moments just to sit and be in touch e wonderful Power that is your spiritual energy. Sit for half a minute or so and do this.

BREAK
At this time, I would like to share with you something you can concentrate on a bit in the coming week. And that is KINDNESS.

See how, when, and if, and how many times you use or could use KINDNESS.

Kindness can be defined by looking into your dictionary. Kindness can also be defined by a feeling within yourself. You know what it is and how to use it clearly.

Pay attention to kindness to yourself, to other people . ..

Now, I do not mean you must go around forgetting your responsibility, but sometimes just a kind smile in a glance and a word or two go a long way. Pay attention to your Self first, then observe your kindness as another key to your own Energy, to your own Personality.

Every week, when we give you a tip or something to concentrate on for a while, it is not simply to have fun with, but because you need to learn to use the tools and this is the way to attain them.

So, kindness shall be the lesson for this week.

A question came up of a news item that week about a violent crime in which the comments were the deviant "couldn't help it" because he might have been "possessed" by the devil.

The questioner asked is there a
reason a man would have no
control over his acts and the
devil possessed him so therefore
is it all right?

The answer is that in some cases
man chooses not to deal with his
own Reality, but instead will
create a fantasy in . . his actions,
his responsibility to his Being,
for creating choices, actions and
reactions from those choices are
so.

Or in some cases, it is very definitely an imbalance of the mental nature. But, of course, as you very well know, there is no existence of a devil. What is in existence are situations, one might say, let us look at it this way: you are a negative person and you are always looking at the bad side of things . . . you are always looking at how bad things are . . . how mean people are, how angry you are . . . Then, what are you creating? You are creating negative energy. Do you not think that negative energy has a power of its own? Of course it does! Thought has power, spiritual

Being has power . . . so the negative energy, as well as positive energy, creates its own power. One could say the habits and patterns that one has created over their life or lives of negativity, anger, resentment and whatever other goodies they want to throw in there – those things can absolutely create an energy of their own. Now, they don't control the Being, but certainly create an effect on the Being – and thereby the Being may feel he is possessed by evil or with another person; when all it is is his Outer Self that he himself has created . . . but it is a negative energy. So, in some cases when you find a mental illness and . . . man will soon find mental illness is a combination of many factors and some are psychic and misdiagnosed with mental trouble – but there are many factors . . . chemical, nutrition, physical and emotional needs. Some cases are a desire not to confront the Truth – not to "see", not to take "responsibility" for one's actions. On the other hand, in some cases the person, the individual, has a lack of connection in the brain stem, which creates a reaction in the body and not connecting the nerves to certain areas in the brain center. This can throw the body out of balance, the emotions out of balance . . . the mental Self out of balance. Research does need to take place in that area of the mental patients' brain stem area.

Also, a chemical reaction is possible in some mental disabilities . . . whether it be to drugs, whether it be to medications, or improper nutrition which is also very important in mental patients because they may not have money for the proper food and diet essentials. Then, the organs, the kidneys, the gall bladder, these organs, the liver . . . all of these create acid conditions in the body . . . all of them secrete, and a little bit too much of one thing and not enough of the other can throw the body into chaos. An older woman friend of mine who lived to be 100 years old, told me she takes a splash of

apple vinegar and a dip of honey
in a cup of hot tea every morning
for her secretions of acid and has
lived without stomach trouble
all her life. Now that could be a
factor. Also, Sassafras tea is good
and marshmallows or
marshmallow root with a few
other herbs good for digestion
will help the physical/mental
balance. But you see there are
many things to take into
consideration. However on the
whole, when one says "the devil
did it and he or she or me is
"possessed" one of two things it
can be . . . absolute fear, feeling
that yes definitely I have guilt
from earlier in my life, so to
speak. Or it could be a pattern

that was established in their ever
overcoming religious beliefs
which is so hard to cure in
mental patients . . . that is, as
they get older and then choose
no longer to see true reality . . .
to face Reality . . . then they use
those things such as the devil
done did it!

So you see, there is no devil,
only the one that man makes for
himself out of negative energy
people so wrongfully use.

Another question which often comes up is whether there is authenticity in the Christian Bible or relevancy to modern times.

The answer came, "yes, of course!"

(END)